D1492547

TIMES REMEMBERED

TIMES REMEMBERED

GEORGE MURRAY ANDERSON

ANCHOR PUBLICATIONS

ISBN 0 984016 23 X

Published and Printed by
ANCHOR PUBLICATIONS
BOGNOR REGIS
GREAT BRITAIN

This book is dedicated to Alastair, my son,
to his wife and my grandchildren on whom
my mantle has fallen.

TIMES REMEMBERED

Preserve me, please, throughout the ages
From over-thumbed and tattered pages.

G.M.A.

GEORGE MURRAY ANDERSON

PREFACE

The interest shown by so many readers in his book "From the Glens to the Lowlands" has encouraged Mr. George Murray Anderson to write a sequel. This continues his reminiscences of a lifetime of farming under varying conditions which, in many respects, have borne little relation to each other.

The result is contained in the following pages. These comments are based on the assumption that the reader is familiar with the previous book.

Part of this volume is concerned with Perthshire where he farmed at one time. This is an area of Scotland that he knows well and loves. The accounts of his subsequent visits, which are interspersed with snatches of history and anecdote, contain descriptions of aspects of the countryside that only a writer of his discernment can appreciate.

Although, in terms of farming years, the scales of his life are now tipped in favour of East Anglia, Mr. Anderson remains a true Scot. He has that capacity for adventure, combined with an aptitude for innovation that has enabled so many of his fellow-countrymen to succeed all over the world. The manner in which he accepted the change from the Scottish Glens to the relative flatness of East Anglia typifies that spirit and this is reflected in these reminiscences. His success in weathering the difficult period between the Wars is evidence of that determination and skill, and these qualities have now been applied to his writings in retirement.

His knowledge of agriculture in general and, in particular, Sheep Rearing and Suffolk Horses is profound. These activities have led, as one would expect, to the field of Judging and Dog Handling and his reputation in these spheres is widely known. He has, however, made no attempt to indulge in descriptions of unusual situations in order to make a story. The success of his first book is evidence of this.

Mr. Anderson's refreshing style will ensure that this book

is read in the spirit in which it is written. A comparison of the styles of life recorded illustrate the changing nature of farming and his perseverance and ability to overcome difficulties in his early days are an inspiration.

The young farmer of today, although faced with differing economic conditions, will benefit from Mr. Anderson's writings.

C W Leverett

"Woodlands"
Debach
Woodbridge
Suffolk

ACKNOWLEDGEMENTS

The author gratefully acknowledges the help of the following in the writing of this book and permission to use photographs

Miss E J Atkinson, O.B.E.
Miss V B Short
Mr C W Leverett, O.B.E., C.St.J.
Miss M B Creasey, for typing the manuscript
Mr G Botfield
Mr A Edmondson
Mr T Glen
Mrs M Glen
Mrs G T Marris
Mrs N Hatcher
Mr D I Alston, C.B.E
Mr T Black
Mr D Lister
Mr H Lacy Scott, O.B.E
Mrs N Harvey
Mrs J Allen Bush
Mrs S Cranston
Mr William Bryson
Mr Robin Laing
Mr Rox
Mr M E Becher
Mr P Flatman
Mr Jack Spence
Mr P Adams
    The Scottish Farmer
    The Southern Reporter
    The East Anglian Daily Times
    The Charles Murray Memorial Trust

CONTENTS

CHAPTER

CHAPTER 1

CHILDHOOD ON A BORDER HILLSIDE

We cannot halt the march of time,
Nor stay the passing years,
A search for lasting youthfulness,
Can only end in tears.
But memory can span the years,
And to our mind recall,
The days of youth and loving friends,
Such memories never pall.

During the first six years of my life the trickling of water was music to me. Born high up on the Cheviot Range where tiny streamlets abound, my wanderings at this age found me never far from the sound of a brook making its way round bends and over stony beds to reach the Arks burn which ran the full length of the hirsel of Border Cheviot sheep which my father tended.

When crossing the Carter Bar the ridge of the Arks edge, the source of the streamlets, can be seen for miles. On and on runs that Border burn to join the river Jed and in turn the Teviot, finally swelling the silvery Tweed. From its springs that wee burn passes through beautiful Border country, from the sunny hillsides through the wooded glades around Jedburgh, under the bridge at Kelso with its famous square to the broad fertile valley between Coldstream and the sea at Berwick. I feel proud to have been born in Scotland, and while I do not regret my present lot, the Borders have aye been dear to me. In my case Scotland has proved to be a grand place to get out of, this may seem strange but it is true. Indeed this is not unusual as many Scots have sought their living in countries throughout the world and on the high seas. From early childhood I have suffered from asthma, and a more equable mild climate has proved beyond

1

doubt beneficial to my health.

Memories of my childhood compel me to linger. The Arks, my home, was more of a farmhouse than a shepherd's cottage. The household consisted of my mother and father, we three brothers and there was an apprentice shepherd boy of 14 years who had just left school, who shepherded the hoggets on the hill known as the Swinlawhope under my father's supervision. Mother had a girl of 14 years to help her in the house, one Mary Scott, the daughter of a shepherd, who was a real pal to us three boys. The sheep on the Border hills are generally Cheviots and Scotch Blackfaces, both hardy breeds and most suitable for these hills, the habitat of the ewes until they are six years of age, having had five crops of lambs. After this time they are sold to lowland farmers for another crop of lambs or for fattening.

The weather in April on the Cheviot Range can be very stormy, with rain and sleet driven by a strong wind. This can be devastating in the lambing season which starts about the middle of the month. April can bring some of the worst weather of the winter. The late G R Rodger of Glen Isla knew all about it when he wrote with a touch of humour,

> The cauldest April e'er I saw
> And many have I seen
> Fierce blizzards blaw wi' driving snaw
> There's nothing growin' green.
> The peesies* cow'r beneath the blast
> And shelter 'mongst the saigs
> They wonder what the devil's wrang
> They should be layin' eggs.

> * lapwings

On the other hand April can bring a nice spell of mild sunny weather. In readiness for bad weather Mother always provided a comfortable "lamb bag" for Father to carry; it was made from closely woven sacking lined with a blanket with a strap for going over the head and shoulder and it was worn under his mackintosh. In the bag he would put any new-born lamb that, owing to the stormy weather, had become cold and seemed likely to perish. Mary Scott was an expert at reviving chilled lambs. When father would bring them into the kitchen, their tender little bodies showing only the slightest signs of life, Mary would set about massaging them in front of a blazing peat fire, stimulating circulation from time to time, and giving them drops of warm milk using a bottle and teat. Life would invariably become evident. When they had fully recovered they would be returned to their mother who usually accepted them. I remember one occasion when an elderly lady friend of my mother's was staying with us for a few days in the lambing season. On the second day of her stay a storm blew up.

> "The wind blew 'as 'twad blawn its last,
> The rattling showers rose on the blast."

Father rushed back from the hill and handed over to Mary two lambs from his lamb bag more dead than alive. "Surely Mary is much too young to be able to deal with these" said the old lady. This immediately aroused the blood in wee Mary's veins. "What," she said, "Do you mean to think that I dinna ken how to fettle a cauld lamb" and she got on with the job. How many lambs Mary saved, I will never know.

We three boys were in close proximity to farm animals. Besides sheep we had cows, calves, pigs, hens and chickens, geese and ducks besides pet rabbits and half a dozen white fan-tailed pigeons and of course three Border Collies. Of all these animals the lovely white Cheviot lambs were our favourites. When I was still a toddler not yet three years old, Mary tried to teach me nursery rhymes. The one I liked best was "Mary had a little lamb" but in the Scottish dialect.

> Mary had a wee, wee lamb
> Its oo* was white as snaw
> And everywhere that Mary gaed**
> The lamb gaed an a'.

> *wool
> **went

My father took great interest in the breeding as well as the shepherding of the Cheviot flock under his charge, and he always tried to get a really good quality sire to mate with his best ewes, so the progeny was likely to be outstanding. One such ram was called "Jock the Jumper", suitably named! So that he did not get to the ewes until the middle of November, my father shut him up in the "Auld Hoose" which stood some sixty yards back from the dwelling house. No doubt it had been the farmhouse hundreds of years before, the old roof having been replaced by one of corrugated iron. Jock was fed on meadow hay and crushed oats during his confinement. It was chiefly to inspect the progeny of "Jock the Jumper" that father invited an old retired shepherd to come and spend a couple of days with him in July. What a time they had selecting likely prize-winning lambs for the forthcoming local show. Early on the afternoon of the second day his friend bade my father goodbye and good luck as he set out for home. As he walked down the hill he met the ewes and lambs grazing gently on their way to the top. He at once got his eye on a lamb he thought he had not previously seen so he returned to tell my father of his discovery and eventually decided to stay another night; what interest and enthusiasm!

Those pleasant memories of the Arks of eighty years ago are all that remain, at least so it seems. Gone is that living community; domestic animal life no longer exists, afforestation has taken control; the brightness has gone from the scene and there is little more than the dark gloom of the pine trees.

The Arks where I lived as a young boy.

CHAPTER II

WIDER HORIZONS

In the spring of 1901 my father moved to North Northumberland so school on the higher reaches of the North Tyne valley was my next experience. Mixing with the local children I learned to talk the Geordie language and I have been able to sound the letter 'R' of the alphabet ever since. It is in this valley that we find the famous Kielder Water, officially opened by the Queen on 26th May 1982. Shortly after the end of the first World War many thousands of acres of hill land, the property of the Duke of Northumberland, were taken over by the Forestry Commission and planted with trees. Nearly sixty years afterwards 1,500,000 trees had to be felled for the vast sheet of water which extended over an area greater than Ullswater and is contained by a dam three quarters of a mile long and 170 feet high. The original estimate for the building of the dam was £38,000,000 but I understand it cost much more. What a transformation of the locality from the days when I attended Kielder School!

From the source of the North Tyne river high up on Deadwater Fell far down the valley to Hexham, sheep grazed in their thousands. Cattle too, raised in this hilly environment, were very popular with the lowland farmers for fattening on their more fertile land. The production of cattle and sheep in this area was responsible for the reputation of at least two people, who with very contrasting interests became household names throughout the valley. They both lived in the village of Stannersburn. Isaac Dagg, a judge of cattle, knowledgeable and trustworthy as a dealer, placed many hundreds of store cattle from this area, these cattle having the reputation of being "great doers". Farmers from a wide lowland area would apply to Isaac to fill their cattle yards for the winter months. Tom Pigg was the other well known personality: he made the famous shepherds' boots, constructed on the full sprung last making them most suitable for walking on steep land. Tom's business extended over a very wide area and although he employed several experienced hands to help him he was apt to get behind in the fulfilling of his orders. The story goes, that a shepherd who had written several letters pleading for his new boots without success, made a final effort in January when the hills were covered in snow, assuring Tom it was damn cold going barefoot. He got his boots in a few days.

A double track railway, now gone, ran from Newcastle the length of the valley and on into Scotland; one can scarcely imagine that so many transformations could occur in the course of a lifetime. The scenery along the banks of that eight-mile-long reservoir will be improved, however, when all the proposed tourist attractions are developed. "Tourists" were coming to this locality in those far off days to which I allude, but they weren't the kind that the authorities try to attract these days. I refer to Gentlemen of the Road. My dictionary gives "tour" as a "prolonged journey from place to place". We children walking the two miles to school would meet as many as ten tourists in a day in ones and twos; some of them we did not like the look of either, especially 'Yorky'. I am well aware that this is not the type of tourist the authorities intend to entertain; the fact is, they do not now exist except perhaps in some of our large towns. The Welfare State has discouraged the activities of these travellers.

I had reached the age of nine, the time most country boys like to be able to whistle by inserting two fingers a little way into the mouth, then blowing. This I could never accomplish until I was well into adult years, though I tried long and often. I just could not make a sound anything like a whistle. However, while yet a boy a young shepherd showed me how to make a whistle from a piece of sucker in spring when the sap had risen in the branches. I always had a sharp pocket knife, except when I happened to lose it. Tom Martin, a friend of the family, would soon find me another supplied by D. D. Deans, Ironmonger, Hawick. I cut a piece of ash sucker about four inches long and being careful not to damage the bark, dipped it in water, then tapped it gently all round with my shut pocket knife so that the bark came off in one piece leaving four inches of nice white wood. At one end I cut the wood on the slant suitable to go between the lips; about three quarters of an inch back from the point I made a deep V-shaped incision about half the depth of the wood. Then from the incision to the point I pared off about one third the depth of the V leaving the surface flat, then replaced the bark, cutting the bark flush with the slope of the wood. I then blew to get a shrill sharp sound.

THE WHISTLE

He cut a sappy sucker from the muckel rodden-tree (1)
He trimmed it, an' he wet it, an' he thumped it on his knee;
He never heard the teuchat (2) when the harrow broke her eggs.
He missed the craggit (3) heron nabbin' puddocks in the seggs,
He forgot to hound the collie at the cattle when they strayed,
But you should hae seen the whistle that the wee herd made!

He wheepled on't at mornin' an' he tweetled on't at nicht,
He puffed his freckled cheeks until his nose sank oot o' sicht,
The kye were late for milkin' when he piped them up the closs,
The kitlins got his supper syne, an' he was beddit boss; (4)
But he cared na doit (5) nor docken what they did or thocht or said,
There was comfort in the whistle that the wee herd made.

For lyin' lang o' mornin's he had clawed the caup (6) for weeks,
But noo he had his bonnet on afore the lave had breeks;
He was whistlin' to the porridge that were hott'rin' on the fire,

8

He was whistlin' ower the travise (7) to the bailie in the byre;
Nae a blackbird nor a mavis, that hae pipin' for their trade,
Was a marrow for the whistle that the wee herd made.

He played a march to battle, it cam' dirlin' through the mist,
Till the halflin' squared his shou'ders an' made up his mind to 'list;
He tried a spring for wooers, though he wistna what it meant,
But the kitchen-lass was lauchin' an' he thocht she maybe kent;
He got ream an' buttered bannocks for the lovin' lilt he played.
Wasna that a cheery whistle that the wee herd made?

He blew them rants sae lively, schottisches, reels, an' jigs,
The foalie flang his muckle legs an' capered owre the rigs,
The grey-tailed futt'rat (8) bobbit oot to hear his ain strathspey,
The bawd (9) cam' loupin' through the corn to 'Clean Pease Strae';
The feet o' ilka man an' beast gat youkie (10) when he played -
Hae ye ever heard o' whistle like the wee herd made?

But the snaw it stopped the herdin' an' the winter brocht him dool,
When in spite o' hacks an' chilblains he was shod again for school;
He couldna sough the catechis (11) nor pipe the rule o' three,
He was keepit in an' lickit when the ither loons got free;
But he aften played the truant ! 'twas the only thing he played,
For the maister brunt the whistle that the wee herd made!

9

(1) rowan: (2) lapwing ; (3) long-necked; (4) empty; (5) fraction of a penny; (6) scraped the bowl; (7) partition; (8) weasel; (9) hare; (10) itchy. (11) catechism.

About forty years ago I learned to whistle using two fingers; what an advantage in working a Border Collie! Collies respond as a rule much better to whistles than words. In recent years too, since I became old, if I wish to contact any of the farm men who may be busy in the buildings up to 200 yards away when they hear one shrill blast they know I want someone. I find the whistle very handy in the Brussel Sprouts trimming season, which is generally from the third week in October to Christmas. I get many telephone calls from people asking for sprouts. As the trimming shed where fifty women and men are busy is not far away, one shrill whistle generally summons the foreman - Paul Watson, to the telephone, so I do not need to leave the house.

CHAPTER III

"YORKY"

Towards the end of the last century, and for 33 years in the present, a notorious tramp called Yorky roamed throughout the hills and dales of the Border Counties. His name was John Oliver, he was from a good family and had had a University education, but unfortunately took to drink and was disowned by his family. It was his frightening appearance and his general rude manner which made him so memorable. A well built man with a strong voice, he would start shouting on entering a village, terrifying women and children. He would decorate himself in the most weird manner in a clutter of coats on which he hung old tins which rattled as he walked; on his head a wide-brimmed tweed hat such as shepherds used to wear, on which he had stuck many fishing flies.

One of his quaint habits was always to walk in the middle of the road because he believed he had the right to occupy the middle of the King's Highway. Cars and buses sounded their horns expecting him to move to the side of the road. He paid not the slightest attention and expected them to go carefully round him. I am afraid he would not have survived long in today's traffic. At times he would settle to work; he had evidently been taught to shear sheep as on the Northumberland side of the Border he was known as the "Daft Clipper". In the next county he was known as the "Durham Ranger". He spent most of the summer months fishing in rivers and burns of the Borders, generally accompanied by a collie dog.

His technique in the border hills was to keep well out of sight of a shepherd's cottage until just after 3 o'clock in the afternoon when the shepherd would leave his house to go round his sheep on the hill. Yorky would then march boldly up to and into the house, sit down and demand his tea. Most shepherd's wives were too scared to refuse to feed him. It was said that he always muttered a Latin grace before his meal to impress the shepherd's wife who reported he could speak Latin. Several people, however, thought that his Latin Grace was a stream of Latin prepositions or prefixes such as we used to learn at school. As harvest drew on he used to help a farmer at Gavinton near Duns in Berwickshire and also stayed for the potato harvest, sleeping in the barn and getting his food at the farm. He once proposed to the farmer's daughter Dolly, who made fun of it. Finally, he celebrated by getting drunk in the town, where a group of boys would follow and tease him; no boy on his own would dare to tackle him, for Yorky would have frightened the very daylights out of him.

> Gie him strong drink until he wink
> That's sunken in despair
> And liquor good to fire his blood,
> That's pressed with grief and care,
> There let him booze in deep caroose
> With bumpers flowing o'er,
> Till he forgets his loves and debts
> And minds his griefs no more.

In collecting information concerning Yorky I have been interested to receive letters from two ladies who, as children, remember seeing him.

Mrs. Nan Harvey of Yetholm remembered that her Granny gave him food. Mrs. Janet Allen Bush who as a child lived with her parents in Duns, recalls what a great event it was when Yorky and his dog came to town. She remembers the boys, including her elder brother, calling after him "Yorky Yorky" and Yorky not liking it. Yorky instilled a sort of fear into her and this was greatly emphasised when one summer's day she set off to visit her grandfather and aunt at Nesbit Lodge. As she turned towards Nesbit, over a dip in the road, she recognised Yorky and his dog coming towards her. She quickly made up her mind to hide behind the broom bushes up a little bank. Here she crouched until the sound of his footsteps on the road died away. "After my grandfather and aunt's pleasure at seeing me, they asked if I had met Yorky. I told them about hiding behind the broom,

YORKY

but their smiles put me at ease. How I wish now I had walked on and met him. I am sure this Gentleman of the Road would have had a kindly word for a child." I have also received a photograph of Yorky and his dog from Mrs. Cranston of Lindean taken by her sister. My thanks to Mrs. Cranston for her kind help.

In the first decade of this century the youthful Mr. Rox lived at Lambden and Hardacres and very often had the opportunity of seeing Yorky at close quarters. He frequently turned up at Hardacres where the Thorburn family always provided him with a meal and he slept in one of the farm buildings. Mr. Rox says Yorky depended a great deal on the goodwill of the Border people and took full advantage of it. Mr. Rox, too, remembers an incident in 1907 or 1908 when he attended Eccles School. One day the class was being taught by a young woman teacher when Yorky strode in accompanied by his dog and demanded a piece of chalk with which to write on the blackboard. The teacher retreated to the other room to fetch the Headmaster who soon appeared and politely but firmly escorted Yorky outside. This short interlude was much appreciated and enjoyed by Mr. Rox and his class mates.

Mr. William Bryson of Earlston has written to tell me about some of Yorky's tricks. He was certainly artful if he thought he could get away with it, especially to housewives, demanding food for himself and his dog. He was a great fisher and had a fisher's book containing no end of valuable flies worth pounds. He also possessed fishing rods, basket and landing net. It was said at the time of his death that a shepherd on the Cheviot Hills got his fishing tackle. There was a story told about him being at Westruther Mains, in the Lammermuirs. One night, he went into the stable to sleep and when the men went there in the morning, Yorky was standing between the hind legs of a cart horse with an arm around each leg. The horse was a kicker. One of the farm chaps said, "Of course you know a wicked animal won't touch a human being of a similar nature." Mr. Bryson believes he could well have been the last person to see Yorky alive. It was on a Friday night when walking to Ladyflat to see his sister, that he heard a shout from the roadside. This was one of Yorky's frightening tricks when he heard footsteps in the dark. He was aware of this and at once made out the seated figure of Yorky. Mr. Bryson was living at Fogorig at the time and on the Sunday morning he recalls the cattleman telling him and his father that Yorky had been found dead at Fogo East End on the Saturday. Mr. Bryson had attended the same school as Mr. Rox, but some five years later, at the time when Yorky was well known. The last word goes to him for he says "Yorky was able to give us a run for our lives and if he couldn't then his dog certainly could."

I am most grateful to Mr. Jack Spence of Duns for the photograph of Yorky's tombstone. Mr. Spence informs me he often saw Yorky at his father's smithy at Darenchester, a village in Berwickshire. A number of tramps would gather there for warmth, some would be allowed to stay overnight, providing they handed over their matches and pipe. Yorky flatly refused, he always seemed to be in a bad temper.

For well nigh half a century Yorky led a wanderer's life, which ended at the beginning of December 1933. He was found in an outhouse on the farm of Fogo East End, he was 83 years of age. Death was stated to have been caused by drinking a poisonous disinfectant. He left a note directing that his collie should be sent to an address in Northumberland, believed to be that of a person from whom he was in the habit of receiving food and shelter. However, I have been told that the dog had to be destroyed before anyone could get near the body. In spite of his wayward habits, some good Samaritan, apparently the Earl of Home's late father, had seen that the wayfarer had a decent burial, which took place in Fogo Churchyard.

The tombstone reads:

HERE LIES
JOHN OLIVER
A WANDERER THROUGHOUT THE BORDERLAND
WHO DIED AT FOGO EAST END
ON 9TH DECEMBER 1933
REST IN PEACE

Yorky's Tombstone

CHAPTER IV

THE YOUNG SHEPHERDS

James Hogg the Ettrick Shepherd wrote:

> Come a' ye jolly shepherd lads
> That whistle through the Glen,
> I'll tell ye a secret that courtiers dinna ken.
> What is the greatest bliss that the tongue of man can name,
> It's to love a bonnie lassie when the cows come hame.

It was common practice throughout the hill land of the Borders for shepherds to keep two cows as a perquisite. These grazed on the hills amongst the sheep he tended so they were apt to stray over a wide area and often returned to the cottage at a late hour to be milked by the shepherd's wife or daughter. I have no doubt it was this experience that prompted James Hogg to write these lines. It has been said that as a young man he was attracted by a "bonnie lassie" over the watershed to the head of Eskdalemuir. In winter I have no doubt he made his visits when the moon was full, there was no artificial lighting to guide one in the darkness over the hills in those days.

In 1905 while I was yet a school boy my father moved into a similar locality to that shepherded by James Hogg, near the Slitrig river which dances down the Glen to meet the Teviot water at Hawick. The farm was owned by Mr. William Elliot whose son Walter later became Minister of Agriculture in a Conservative Government. We lived a mile from Shankend Station where passenger and goods trains ran every half hour on the Carlisle to Edinburgh route. Now the thirteen bay viaduct near the Station is the only construction left to remind one that trains once ran that way. The 8.20 am took me to school in Hawick a long long

The House at Pleaknowe where I lived when a schoolboy

time ago. Soon my school days were over, though I had more days than most. At that time as a rule children left at the age of fourteen years; with the help of a birthday my schooling continued until I was fifteen years of age. After that we moved into a beautiful valley four miles from Yetholm, at the top was the purple-headed mountain known at 'The Gyle'. Some six miles lower where we lived the Bowmont river flowed gently by.

Early in my life as a shepherd boy, attending sheep sales and agricultural shows, I got to know many Border shepherds; though they were mostly many years my senior, they were so friendly they gave their advice freely on matters I wished to know more about.

Throughout my long farming career the breeding of a variety of animals I thought suitable to the likely production the farm was capable of has been a great pleasure to me. I started with the famous Border Cheviots; how proud I was to win my first prize for a gimmer at the Yetholm Border Shepherds' Show, away back in 1911.

While I was yet a herd laddie I was instructed to drive 120 lambs with my Border Collie, Fly, to the farm of Fans near Earlston, Berwickshire. I started from the Bowmont valley four miles above Yetholm and arrived at Spylaw Farm on the outskirts of Kelso that evening. The farmer was a Mr. Scott with whom arrangements had been made for grazing for the lambs overnight, Fly and I staying with the shepherd. On turning off the Yetholm to Kelso Road into Spylaw Farm drive one passed under an arch, the sides of which were the jawbones of a whale set wide enough apart to allow farm traffic to pass. The jaws were joined at the top by a hard piece of wood, probably oak. On returning home I remember telling my friends that I had driven a flock of sheep through the jaws of a whale! Next day I made an early start so I got through the town of Kelso before there was much traffic, then the lambs became very tired and were only able to travel at less than two miles an hour. Eventually I arrived at Fans, farmed in those days by an elderly gentleman called Mr. Herbertson; he took charge of the lambs and invited me in to tea. How refreshed I was when I set out to walk the few miles to St. Boswells station where I caught the last passenger train for Kelso. Bobby Mercer with his horse-drawn waggonette always met that train so Fly and I got safely back to Yetholm; we had then only four miles to walk home. Today this method of moving sheep appears so ancient; 72 years ago there was no other way.

I found the noted flock of Cheviot sheep in my father's care most interesting, shepherding them seemed more a way of life than the fact that one was working for a living. Then suddenly the First World War of 1914-18 started a bitter struggle against the Germans. Our daily newspapers showing long lists of killed and wounded were most depressing to everyone. There was also at home the unexpected death of my father in 1916, on his hill in the lambing season. He was suffering from 'flu but insisted on seeing to his sheep. My elder brother by this time had joined the forces, the Kings Own Scottish Borderers. My brother Frank and I were then left in charge of this large flock of Cheviot ewes and rams. While we had had a good grounding in the management of sheep we felt we were left to fight our own battles in the world and use what abilities we had, together with any God-given talents we were lucky enough to possess. We were glad to benefit from experienced friends.

I remember so well that we were preparing some thirty Cheviot rams for the Hawick Ram Fair but about a month before the sale a number developed sores on their heads. We tried various remedies but without success. We became very worried indeed as time was running short. One day I drove, with my Border Collie Nell, sixty lambs to a grass field rented at Clifton Park about six miles away; the road led by Linton Burnfoot farm where luckily I met Tom Purvis the Shepherd. I told him of the trouble we were having with the rams. "I think I have something that will cure them," said Tom, "It's called rock bluestone." He also told me how to apply it. "Call at my cottage on your way back," said Tom, "I'll have some wrapped up." It certainly cured the trouble, by sale time the sores had completely healed and the hair had started to grow. If anyone at the sale noticed the rams had had any trouble they did not mention it to me and all the rams made good prices.

At about that time the government of the Falkland Islands approved the purchase from Messrs. Andrew Oliver and Sons, Auctioneers, Hawick, of some ten or fifteen

My home as a young herd in the cottages behind
the steading and house at Attonburn, Yetholm

Cheviot rams with the particular request that their wool must be of the finest quality. From the glimpses we have recently seen on television I see that the breed of sheep on the islands appear to have white faces. They are probably the descendants of that consignment of rams despatched from Hawick Tup Fair before the First World War. Following the recent war with Argentina, perhaps the time has come to replenish the Falkland Islanders' livestock with a further consignment of Cheviot rams from the high Border hills. Fresh blood would instil additional vigour into these flocks and I doubt if any breed would be more suitable for such wild stormy islands.

During the eight years I lived in the Bowmont valley two great disasters occurred, the 1914-18 World War with its unbelievable massacre of human lives, followed by a foreign type of 'flu which claimed probably as many deaths throughout the world as the terrible War. May I say I had reached the age to join the forces but as I was engaged in the production of food and as head shepherd of a sizeable flock I was exempt from being called up. One spring towards the end of that war J Logie Robertson wrote these verses:

The thaw has come! The skies are clear
The gowk's (1) been heard - the spring is here
The sweetest time o' a' the year!
The birds are chantin'
An' the fragrant buds are on the brier
An' green leaves cleed (2) the plantin'

Ower the clean land the plooman flings
The rattlin' seed, the Shepherd sings
Beside his flock among the springs
Me the adviser
They wadna change their lot wi' Kings
Wi' Chancellor or Kaiser.

Death stricks athwart the joyous scene,
Transmutes what is to what has been
And with the same unchanging mien
Rigidly callous
Darkens the Cottage on the Green
An' Desolates the palace.

(1) cuckoo; (2) covers.

George the Herd at 21.

CHAPTER V

FAREWELL TO THE BORDERS

On 28th May 1919 I bade goodbye to the beautiful Bowmont Valley. It was exactly twenty years later when on holiday in Scotland, that I arrived in Yetholm and toured the valley I had known so well. The everlasting hills were just as I had left them! As I drove slowly up the side of the Bowmont River many memories, happy and sad, came to mind. My home by then was many miles away in East Anglia.

After leaving the Bowmont Valley we moved to a lone shieling high up on a Border hillside facing east where rays of sun shone on us in the early mornings that lovely first summer. Scotch blackfaced sheep which grazed the heather far up the hill behind the house were early risers and by 6.0 a.m. some of them had already reached the house where they seemed to enjoy the rich green grass close by. Lower down was grassy hill-land stretching to the dry stonewall some 400 yards away; over the wall were pastures where horses, cattle and sheep grazed contentedly together. Frank and I were more free to plan our future, deciding to form a partnership and to rent a farm which we felt we could manage. We knew it would not be easy as we had no previous general farming experience.

However in the meantime we rented two grass fields to stock principally with sheep. At this time I became acquainted with the late Mr. George Davidson and Mr. Tommy Rutherford of the Scottish Mutton Company whose abattoir on the outskirts of Hawick was used for the slaughter of sheep and lambs for the London market. They agreed to accept any lambs we could purchase suitable for their trade. This was an education to me, my judgement as a purchaser on the hoof being checked by the price on the hook the buyer in London was able to pay. The experience I gained over eighteen months has stood me in good stead throughout my long farming career. I am grateful to these two gentlemen for the opportunity they gave me in estimating the value of a fat sheep. I have often been invited to judge fat sheep classes and also various classes of commercial sheep at Agricultural Shows.

Recently, a neighbour who is a member of a Young Farmers' Club told me that he had been chosen to judge fat lambs for his club at a judging competition at the forthcoming Annual County Rally. Could I help him as he had little knowledge on the subject? By this time I had disposed of my sheep so I had no material for a practical demonstration. However I cut out a picture of a sheep, stuck it on a piece of paper and arrowed the three principal parts of a fat sheep. I then wrote the order in which he should describe the lambs and told him not to mention any part not arrowed as time would be limited. He got first prize for judging and a lovely cup to keep for one year. I applaud this young farmer for his ability in making full use of the scanty instructions I was able to give him. One day he may well become a successful producer of fat lambs.

Mother, Frank and I loved the Borders.

I have seen Yarrow's rising sun casting her soft warm light
Over the round green hills and the skylark in his flight,
I have seen the silver of St. Mary's to gold turning
In the peaceful quiet of a still Summer morning.

Now that our minds were made up we hoped we would be successful in renting a farm in or near the county of Roxburghshire. Our hopes and endeavours, however, proved unsuccessful; it was in Perthshire that we were eventually offered the tenancy of a 900 acre hill farm with some thirty acres of arable land in the parish of Glendevon in the Ochil Hills and here we spent the following five years. This decision deprived us of the close association with many Border relations and friends, it also restricted the interest we had long developed in the South Country breed of Cheviot sheep, as Scotch Blackfaces were the recommended breed for grazing the Ochil Hills. However we had the opportunity to farm which was our chief desire. With showers of good wishes on leaving we arrived at our new

Coulsknowe Farm Nr. Glendevon, Perthshire
The house where my brother and I started
farming in 1920.

farm on the 28th November, 1920 and soon made a number of friends, the local people being most kind to us. Prices for all farm products, however, deteriorated disastrously after our first six months at the farm. Consequently we had to scheme and work hard to make the most of a difficult time. We at once set to work to improve the sheepstock by breeding our replacements from our better ewes, by a good ram. We certainly improved the breed of ewe by this method.

Frank and I again suffered sad bereavement by the loss of our dear mother following a stroke. This was a heavy blow to us both. She was laid to rest in the family grave in Morebattle Churchyard six miles from Kelso.

When grey days come and cares abound
And fate with grief your lone heart fills,
Then go where solace can be found
And wander on the quiet hills.

Climb up beyond the grazing sheep
To heights where peace and beauty reign,
Here's space to think in silence deep
And prayer makes well the heart again.

Bright flowers will cheer your homeward way
For peace and silence sooth all ills,
Courage you'll find for another day
While wandering on the eternal hills.

CHAPTER VI

BEAUTIFUL PERTHSHIRE

Perthshire, situated in the very centre of Scotland, none of it reaching the sea, is, in my opinion, the most picturesque of our Scottish Counties. Stretches of productive arable land can be seen from the excellent winding roads which accompany the sparkling rivers on their way to the peaceful lochs, through lovely glens with mountains towering high on either side.

A tourist visiting Scotland for the first time would naturally want to see the capital Edinburgh on the way north. The Royal Mile, the famous Prince's Street and many historical buildings. However it is to Perthshire we are going. There are various routes from Edinburgh and the one I would choose would be by South Queensferry over the Forth Road Bridge and after a mile or so turn left to Dunfermline; then take the road to Powmill, then to Rumbling Bridge and the Yetts of Muckhart; you are then in Perthshire. Yett is the Scottish word for gate. Should you happen to be a sheep farmer and a few of your flock should stray into a beautiful garden, the owner's pride and joy, you might find difficulty in getting the infuriated lady to listen to your humble apologies for the damage your sheep had done, however, when the storm had abated somewhat you could try to suggest that in future she would be wise to shut her yett.

So we enter Perthshire and lovely Glendevon at the Yetts, perhaps not the rugged scenery of the highland part of the county but all the way to the top of the Glen are those green grassy hills rising high on either side of the road with the river Devon flowing by, "Crystal Devon, Winding Devon" as Burns describes it. Those grassy hills produce large quantities of lamb and wool. The sheep are the Scotch Blackfaces, most numerous of any pure breed in Britain.

The village of Glendevon is situated on either side of the river where there are two hotels. The tiny church, one of the smallest in Scotland, has beautiful stained glass windows and the comfortable seating impresses visitors.

I have been told that a toll existed at the Yetts a long time ago and that horse drawn vehicles laden with coal from the coalfields in Fife were the main traffic before railways existed. The sign definitely states Yetts of Muckhart and, as there are crossroads here, the likelihood is that there would have been at least two gates. The road on the left as we approach from Dunfermline leads down to the village of Muckhart and on to Dollar; the one on our right is to the village of Caranbo and on to Milnathort. The one we take is straight over to Glendevon's lovely glen that takes one right through the Ochil Hills to the Stirling to Perth Road. By now perhaps you fancy a cup of coffee; here is the famous Gleneagles Hotel. Step inside and you will enjoy a cup of the best. I have had several. Now we proceed further to the town of Crieff passing through highly productive arable and grass land. Crieff is a good centre from which to visit the Trossachs. Let us start by climbing the hill above Aberfoyle from the Dukes Road. You will enjoy the wonderful view. Loch Vennachar, Loch Chon and Loch Artlet are on the left and beyond the country stretches away to Stronachlachar, Ben Lomond towering high above Loch Ard. For those who love to walk why not visit Royal Cottage, where Queen Victoria in 1859 set the water flowing from Loch Katrine to Glasgow to provide its large population with limitless quantities of clean water. You will also enjoy a sail on this beautiful loch listening to famous tunes played by a Scottish piper.

A visit to Callander is 'a must' though it were only to view from the road 'Arden House', where the programme, Dr. Finlay's Casebook was enacted, giving so much pleasure, especially to us exiles. From Callander we travel north, the road taking us along the side of Loch Lubnaig. Before we get there we hear the Falls of Leny on the river Teith; after heavy rain it can be thrilling to stand and watch the water foaming over the rocks. At the further end of Loch Lubnaig is Strathyre, "Bonnie Strathyre" of the well known Scottish song, with Ben Vorlich rising to a great height. Now we

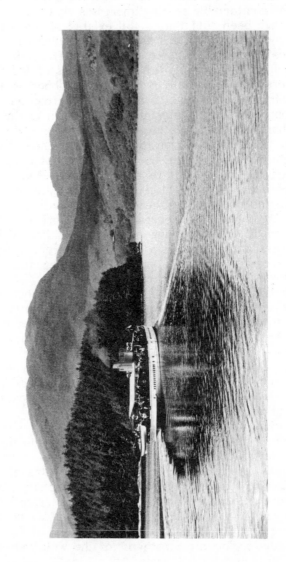

Loch Katrine

approach Balquhidder where Rob Roy MacGregor is buried in the Churchyard. Golden eagles still fly over the braes and there is a long established eyrie by the side of Loch Voil a few miles to the west. Scott wrote:

> "The Eagle he was the lord above
> And Rob the lord below"

Soon we come to Loch Earn; of the roads encircling it we take the first on the right which skirts the base of Ben Vorlich and hugs the south shore. This is a quiet and peaceful road away from buses and tourists' cars. At the east end of the loch is St. Fillans, one of Scotland's prettiest villages. By following the shore of the loch you return to the west end and the village of Lochearnhead, an attractive resort with fishing, water-skiing, sailing, and hills to climb. The road up Glen Ogle runs between these hills and at nearly 1,000 feet one sees more of the rugged Highlands. As you ascend this steep winding Glen you may drive to a lay-by and look across to the mountain opposite, you will be able to detect a track where once a railway ran from Lochearnhead to Crainlarich and on to Oban. What a variety of scenery one can see from this track! To climbers whose headquarters are in this locality and who are not so ambitious as to tackle the steep high mountain, why not, after a stimulating Scotch breakfast of porridge and two eggs with your rashers, walk up Glen Ogle then cross to the old disused railway on the hillside opposite and return to Lochearnhead at your leisure. It is Perthshire I am describing and having ascended Glen Ogle turn right and run downhill to Killin and Loch Tay. There are good hotels in Killin where I have enjoyed staying on several occasions. At the head of the sixteen mile long Loch Tay with Ben Lawers towering on the left lies the way to Fearnen and Fortingall. In company with my friend Morrie on more than one occasion I have enjoyed the beauties of this enchanting part of Perthshire.

> Mountains majestic, in their grandeur
> Soaring proudly towards the sky:
> Sweeping down to slopes more tender
> There we find peace that none can buy.

Loch Earn

Loch Tay and Ben Lawers, Perthshire

Fortingall Village, Perthsire

The Falls of Dochart near Killin

In the pretty village of Kenmore are the lovely iron gates at the entrance of the grounds of Taymouth Castle, once the stately home of the Marquis of Breadalbane.

The Rev. William Gillies, who was minister of Kenmore for many years, gives a comprehensive description and wonderful history of this area and the vast lands of the Marquis of Breadalbane in his book 'Famed Breadalbane' with its touches of humour. Even the Marquis must have been amused when the following verses appeared in Punch:

From Kenmore to Ben Mohr
The land is a' the Marquiss's
The mossy howes, the heathery knowes
An ilka bonnie park is his.

The bearded goats the towzie stots
An' a' the braxy carcasses
Ilk crofters rent ilk tinkers tent
An ilka collies bark is his.

The muir cocks craw the pipers blaw
The gillies hard days work is his
From Kenmore to Ben Mohr
The world is a' the Marquiss's

At the beginning of the 19th century the game bird Capercaillie became nearly extinct in the Highlands of Scotland, however, in 1836 the Marquis of Breadalbane brought forty nine from Sweden and liberated them at Taymouth Castle. Smaller consignments tried previously had failed to multiply, but the Marquis's efforts bore fruit. Twenty five years later he reported he had fully 1,000 birds in the woods and it is from this Taymouth experiment that most of the Capers found in the Highlands today originally came. The cock bird is as big as a turkey, but the flesh of the Caper is said to be inedible. So why shoot it? It feeds chiefly on pine shoots so is no favourite of the Forestry Commission. I have not seen one, but I am told the male is a most handsome bird, its general colour is bluish grey, the breast glossed with green.

To old folks it is wonderful to be able to drive on a

Taymouth Castle

beautiful tarred road over the shoulder of Ben Lawers and to view the landscape from this high altitude, then to drive on into Glen Lyon following the river Lyon. One cannot help noticing the beauty of the trees at this part of the Glen; huge beeches, pine trees, oak, larch, birch, chestnut and rowan trees. Further up the Glen is Meggernie Castle; in the early eighteenth century Meggernie and Chesthill were both owned by James Menzies of Caldare who brought the larch tree to Scotland. Glen Lyon owes most of its fine trees to Menzies and, in my opinion, the wood of the larch tree grown to maturity in Scotland compares well with English oak. You could spend days in Glen Lyon which teems with history and legend. The village of Fortingall is famous for its Yew tree in the churchyard, over 3,000 years old and the oldest in Europe.

Shortly before the birth of Christ the Emperor Augustus sent envoys to Fortingall to meet the Picts and tradition says that one of the legionaries married a Scotch woman who bore him a son who became Pontius Pilate. Glen Lyon is the home of the Campbells, John Campbell who took part in the Massacre of Glencoe building the first stone house here in 1728. Some six miles from Loch Tay the road takes us to the attractive small town of Aberfeldy, one of the most beautiful parts of the Highlands. Here is General Wade's famous bridge over the Tay built by William Adam, the master mason and architect, in 1733, at that time when Wade was quelling the Jacobite rising. A short distance from the bridge is the monument erected in 1887 to mark the raising of the Black Watch, the 42nd Regiment of the Line. The Watch was first raised in 1667 to be in constant guard for securing peace in the Highlands. Their tartan is a very dark one, contrasting with the English red coats at that time hence the name Black Watch. Lovely parks and entertainment grounds abound in the town of Aberfeldy and it is here we find the hillsides covered with the famous Birch trees, "The Birks of Aberfeldy".

The following verses by Scotland's National Poet are a fitting description of this lovely Highland scene:

Now Simmer blinks (1) on flow'ry braes,
And o'er the crystal streamlets plays

Come let us spend the lightsome days
In the birks of Aberfeldy.

The little birdies blythely sing
While o'er their heads the hazels hing (2)
Or lightly flit on wanton wing,
In the birks of Aberfeldy

The braes ascend like lofty wa's (3)
The foaming stream deep-roaring fa's
O'er hung with fragrant-spreading shaws (4)
The birks of Aberfeldy.

(1) shines; (2) hang; (3) walls; (4) woods.

Some fifteen miles from here to the west we come to
Kinloch-Rannoch another centre of real Highland scenery.
Approaching, we pass the base of one of the most shapely
mountains in Scotland, Schiehallion, and from the road one
gets an excellent view of the surrounding locality; from the
village of Rannoch where there are two hotels, roads run on
either side of the Loch. In August with the heather in full
bloom and the water reflecting the sky, where can one find
anything more beautiful and peaceful? The River Tummel
flows out from Loch Rannoch. Let us follow the road that
runs east alongside it to Loch Tummel where we admire the
scenery from the Queen's View, one of the finest in the
country, which Queen Victoria visited in 1866.

From here we continue east to join the Pitlochry to Blair
Atholl road near the Pass of Killiecrankie on the river
Garry. There are beautiful wooded walks here and the
famous Soldiers' Leap about a mile from which the battle of
Killiecrankie was fought in 1689 in a field named Urrard.
The Jacobite victory was turned to disaster by the loss of
their leader Dundee.

I have happy memories of a weekend I spent together
with my friend Tommy Miller at the invitation of Mr. and
Mrs. Peter Cameron, of Monzie, Blair Atholl whose
farmhouse is situated on the lower slopes of Ben-y-Gloe. If I
remember correctly, to reach the house from the main road
one had to cross several pasture fields each enclosed by a
dry stone wall, this necessitated the opening and shutting of

'Soldiers' Leap' spanned by a Jacobite
fleeing from the English after the Battle of Culloden

a number of 'yetts'. To a livestock farmer like myself the opening and shutting of gates was an everyday occurrence so we thought nothing of it. However, this was nearly half a century ago and I wonder if John, who was a small boy at that time and who has now followed his father on the farm, has discovered a less time-consuming way of covering the last mile or so to his home, in these days of invention.

Blair Atholl which lies some seven miles north of Pitlochry where the Garry and Tilt rivers meet, has at least two hotels. There is lovely Highland scenery here with the mountain Ben-y-Gloe, 3,671 feet high, standing slightly to the south and Blair Castle, the home of the Duke of Atholl, a little way north of the village. The Castle, though a private residence, is open to the public at certain times and I found it most interesting and well worth a visit. Tommy Miller and I were much impressed by the improvement to the hill grazing that Peter Cameron had accomplished by cultivating a sizeable acreage on the side of the mountain and re-seeding it with a mixture of permanent grasses and clovers. The reward for Peter's hard work was evident by the healthy appearance of a fine lot of suckler cows and calves which we saw enjoying this sweet, lush grazing. The calves would be sold in the Autumn probably at Perth where, I am sure, they would find a ready buyer. His ewes and lambs, the Scotch Blackface breed, also grazed the mountain and must have found the grass on this large re-seeded area very tasty and sweet compared with the original grasses and heather; they certainly looked in perfect health and condition. Besides their large stock raising farm at Monzie Mr. and Mrs. John Cameron have another interest. Some years ago they acquired the old school in Blair Atholl and I understand that here they have made a very interesting museum, with a number of local animals carefully preserved in lifelike form and many 'bygones' of Highland Perthshire. The 'Scottish Farmer' has published an interesting article about this museum which must be a real holiday attraction. From Blair Atholl let us retrace our steps and continue to Pitlochry, a popular tourist centre, raised to burgh status in 1947. Here many tourist attractions including the Pitlochry Festival Theatre where a wide variety of plays are given during the summer season.

Scotch Blackface sheep feeding on hay from a rack

Besides a tweed mill and two distilleries there is the famous hydro-electric dam 2,700 gallons of water being fed to it daily from Loch Tummel. The salmon ladder is a special interest. Pitlochry is situated near the centre of Scotland in the wooded Tummel valley, and golf, tennis, pony trekking, fishing, skiing and climbing are all attractions. From here we drive South to Dunkeld passing through the village of Logierait where the Tummel and Tay rivers meet. Dunkeld is a delightful little town, on the river Tay, by-passed by the new A9, so there is little heavy traffic in its streets and it is a charming place for a holiday. Over the bridge built by Telfer is Little Dunkeld; from here a road branches to Birnam, a lovely hilly, wooded part. Dunkeld has a Cathedral and the National Trust of Scotland together with the Perth County Council has carried out an improvement programme to some twenty houses, a remarkable example of conservation of seventeenth and eighteenth century County Town houses. Neil Gow, a celebrated eighteenth century fiddler who composed many of the country's famous airs lived here. Dunkeld has a number of excellent hotels. When the 7th Duke of Atholl decided to build a house for his Duchess he chose one of the finest sites in Scotland, the house being finally completed in 1900. For the last forty years it has been Dunkeld House Hotel situtated some distance from the village and surrounded by grounds of great beauty. As we leave, it is now twelve miles to Perth.

Perth well deserves to be called "the Fair City", situated as it is on the winding banks of the Tay with fine buildings and the spacious North and South Inches, beautiful parks which young and old alike can enjoy. The Art Galleries are well worth a visit and of course, all who know Sir Walter Scott's "Fair Maid of Perth" will want to see the "Fair Maid's House" behind which was the Blackfriars Monastery where James I was murdered despite the efforts of Catherine Douglas to hold the door with her arm when it was found that the bar was missing. For two hundred years until 1948 the Black Watch had their headquarters in the Queen's Barracks. To appreciate fully the beauties of Perth and its surroundings, visitors should climb Kinnoull Hill. At its foot stretches the fertile agricultural lands of the Carse of Gowrie reaching to the outskirts of Dundee and through it all flows that fine salmon river, the Tay. Perth has one of the largest livestock markets in Britain. All classes of cattle, sheep and pigs come here from a very wide area and buyers from abroad come to purchase breeding stock. One of my farming friends in Suffolk takes his pedigree Simmental bulls to sell in this market. In the summer months during the years I farmed in Perthshire, I sometimes sold my lambs at this centre. As I was seventeen miles away and in those days no motor transport was available for livestock, the lambs had to be driven by road, with the help of a well trained border collie. This was not difficult as there was not the amount of traffic there is today. It took two days for the journey, travelling ten miles the first day and about seven on the morning of the sale. A kind farmer near the village of Forteviot let me rest my lambs in one of his meadows overnight, as he did for my neighbours who were also driving their lambs by road. We stayed at the local inn and the innkeeper kindly saw that our dogs were fed. After disposing of our lambs at the sale we returned home from Perth station in the late afternoon to Rumbling Bridge, via Kinross, the dogs travelling in the compartment at no extra charge. Being well trained they crawled under the seats of the compartment and were no trouble to anyone. After alighting at Rumbling Bridge we had three miles to walk arriving home about 7.30 p.m. Today lambs are transported that distance in little over an hour, the farmer coming along to the sale later in his car.

A short distance from Perth's Queens Bridge on the Blairgowrie Road stands Scone palace (pronounced Scoon) the home of the Earl of Mansfield. The palace is open to the public at certain times of the year and is one of the most historic places in Scotland. The present Lord Mansfield is the Minister responsible for Agriculture in Scotland. The Stone of Destiny was brought to Scone from either Dunstaffnage or Iona during the reign of Kenneth MacAlpine who, in AD 843, united the Picts and Scots into a single kingdom. The Kings of Scotland were crowned upon it at Scone. The stone was stolen by King Edward I of England and thereafter it became part of the Coronation Chair in Westminster Abbey. The Stone is a rectangular block of red sandstone, twenty-six by sixteen by ten inches, and may have been a portable altar belonging to a Celtic ecclesiastic or missionary. From Scone we keep travelling north to Blairgowrie, a fertile district well known for the growing of raspberries. Scotland's most picturesque Golf Course is quite near at Rosemont.

From Blairgowrie we travel on to the Bridge of Cally and to Glenshee where there is a skiing resort. A short distance further on we come to the Devil's Elbow, a very steep twisting road which is often blocked by snow in winter, and eventually leads to Braemar, but that is in Aberdeenshire.

Meikleour is a village near the Blairgowrie to Perth road in which stands the mansion home of the Marquis of Lansdown, which was enlarged by David Bryce in 1869. The grounds are magnificently planted, the great feature being the beech hedge that stretches for 580 yards along the road. The beech trees were planted in 1746 and have now attained a height of 90 feet; the hedge is pruned at regular intervals the operation being a major undertaking. Having lived for five years in the county and visiting it many times since then, I have tried to describe regions which are accessible by car, having long since ceased to be either a hiker or a climber.

The Beech Hedge, Perthshire

CHAPTER VII

MOVE TO EAST ANGLIA

The beginning of the last year of the tenancy of our farm in Glendevon was fast approaching. My brother and I felt we must seek "pastures new" so a letter was sent to the Agent in Edinburgh to say we had decided to terminate the tenancy of the farm in November 1925. This gave us a year in which to find a future home. Soon information reached us that a number of farmers were leaving Ayrshire and Lanarkshire for East Anglia, where it was said opportunities for farmers were more encouraging. By the kindness of our friend Willie Sinclair we were put in touch with Arthur Forbes who had already farmed in Norfolk for several years. This introduction saw us heading South in the latter part of October of that year. Before this however, I married Edith Rankin from the Lammermuirs; this proved to be a happy partnership for over fifty years. There is no doubt that people moving from the hills and glens of Scotland to a very different environment such as East Anglia, for a time at least, miss the green and heathery hills and the running burns. There are no hills and the streams of East Anglia meander slowly along. It may be of interest to some readers that of all the thirty years I lived in Scotland for twenty-five of that time I suffered from asthma. Shortly after I arrived in East Anglia I found the trouble had completely gone, the warmer air and milder winters compared with the colder ones in Scotland had effected the cure.

During our early years in East Anglia we made Bury St. Edmunds our chief market town where I attended regularly each Wednesday except for two weeks during the lambing season and two weeks at harvest. Bury, as it is generally known, is situated in the Western part of Suffolk and is surrounded by a wide area of useful arable land, only a small percentage of the area being in grass. Consequently Bury market is a large one, a number of firms taking part. Messrs. Simpson and Sons sell the majority of the fat cattle and the fat sheep. Messrs. Lacy Scott and Sons sell the store cattle and calves; they also share the pig market with Messrs. Chevell Lawrence and Sons, each firm generally selling over a thousand head every week, store and fat pigs from the age of about eight weeks to old fat sows and boars. Many fat pigs are bought here for the London trade, they are sold in numbers up to eight and ten in a pen; only sows and boars are sold singly.

Messrs. Lacy Scott and Sons have large sales of all classes of breeding sheep and lambs during the summer months. They consist of shearling ewes, older ewes, lambs for fattening and stock besides various breeds of rams. One sheep sale is held in July another in August and the third in September, numbers ranging from twelve to fourteen thousand at each sale. They are the largest sales in East Anglia. I have bought and sold many sheep at these sales over the years.

There is also an auction sale for poultry and eggs at Bury conducted by Abbott, Gooding and Sons where my wife sold her eggs each week. The same firm sold tame and wild rabbits, ferrets, pheasant and partridge in their season, pigeons and ornamental ducks. Later in the day the Corn Exchange opened. This was a large building near the centre of the town where there were many rows of single stands, each one having its representative. There were grain buyers for wheat, barley and oats, agents for feeding stuffs, artificial manure agents, insurance agents, buyers and sellers of all classes of grass seeds and clovers. Besides a number of agents for farm machinery there was also a stand where one could order cattle medicine and so on.

In 1938, after I moved to the Boulge Hall Farm, Ipswich was my weekly market, conducted each Tuesday on similar lines to that at Bury St. Edmunds. By attending markets, serving on agricutural committees, taking part in the running of one's local shows and many other friendly gatherings the ordinary farmer benefits from the many interesting and knowledgeable people he meets. I would like to recall some personalities I have knows as outstanding farmers and businessmen in their day.

JAMES ALSTON OF UPHALL

I was introduced to James Alston by the late Arthur Forbes soon after I arrived in Suffolk. A native of Ayrshire he had farmed in East Anglia many years before I arrived. He had been tenant of the Home Farm at Rougham near Bury St. Edmunds for three years then moved to a farm on Sir Maitland Wilson's Estate at Bardwell and had finally settled at Uphall near Diss. To his 500 acre farm it was not long before he added several more farms making a total of over 1,200 acres. He specialised in dairy cows and sugar beet in which he was most successful. James's interests were not wholly confined to his own farming, he took a keen interest in the public life of the county of Norfolk in which he lived. He worked hard for such organisations as the Norfolk Agricultural Station, the Agricultural Executive Committee, the Milk Committee of the Norfolk branch of which he was Chairman and the Norfolk Branch of the Farmer's Union, being five times chairman. He had an absolute belief in the principles for which the Union stands and the importance to the nation of maintaining a prosperous agricultural industry. Successful as he was in all this, I believe he will be best remembered by the many relations and friends he was instrumental in bringing to East Anglia, between the two wars.

The four course shift of crops had become uneconomic and even ruinous. Mr. Alston and his many Scots farmer friends were to become pioneers of the East Anglia economy of dairying and growing Sugar Beet. It must have been in the sugar beet chopping-out season when Mr. Alston and I were discussing farming topics in Bury Market. I happened to enquire "How many people do you employ these days?" "Sixty-five," was his answer. "However do you manage to look after that lot?" I asked. "Well, it is very important to have good foremen, very important indeed," and he added, with a smile, "I can ride a bike." While I do not class my ability anywhere near that of James Alston I find that we are similar in at least two aspects of our lives. We each had occupied two farms before settling down in the third, in my case Boulge Hall Farm. The other similarity was that we had both done most of our courting by letter, although the

49

James Alston of Uphall

courtships ended slightly differently. He had to go back to Scotland to get his bride, while I brought mine with me. James Alston will be remembered for his knowledge of land and its potential but even more for his service to his fellow men given with kindliness and charm, two features of his fine personality. He died suddenly in April 1958 at the age of 77 years.

DAVID BLACK OF BACTON

David Black was born at New Year Field, Liveston, near Bathgate in 1874. In 1898 he married Katie Sommerville and started farming at Red House Farm, Bacton near Stowmarket Suffolk, a 198 acre farm in poor condition; the first two years he had it rent free. He at once had a big barn converted into a cowshed and brought a herd of Ayrshire cows from Scotland. He was the first farmer in this district to send milk to London and this was put on rail at Finningham Station. At that time and perhaps for several hundred years before, butter was the principal product delivered from the dairy cow. Red Polls were the recognised breed for that purpose as they also produced calves suitable to grow to beef. Farmers' wives would appear at their stands on a street known as Butter Market, deriving its name from the butter industry in those far off days. While Mr. Black never liked cows he put up with them for thirty years.

When David's son Tom became of age his father gave him £100 so that he could start keeping pigs like many other Suffolk farmers in those days. Tom kept a strict balance sheet of this new enterprise with the result that having given it a fair trial he discovered pigs made a nice profit. This gave Mr. Black senior much encouragement and he went headlong into the business of keeping pigs. He built fattening houses for pigs and it was not long before the herd had increased to many hundreds. He experimented in feeding and also in the design of the buildings, as new methods developed, besides building new houses, he would at once bring old buildings up to date until he had 3,000 pigs.

In the depression of 1921 and the years to follow grain prices were very low indeed so Mr. Black bought most of the

David Black of Bacton

food for his pigs, while he turned his own land to other, more profitable crops, increasing his acreage of fruit, apples of different varieties, pears, plums, raspberries and blackcurrants. In 1923 he was approached by a Scottish firm to grow grass seeds for them and soon he was growing 200 acres of Timothy, Fescue, Cocksfoot and other grasses. By now he had bought two more large farms. Other crops grown included sugar beet, potatoes, cabbages and twenty acres of rhubarb, besides plants and flowers for the Covent Garden cut flower trade beginning with daffodils and ending with gladioli. While these crops required a great deal of organisation for production and sale, the pig enterprise continued to be well managed, large numbers of bacon pigs being sent for slaughter each week. It was not until 1939 that the numbers had to be reduced to 500. After the war, numbers started to increase again and soon they were back to three times that number.

All this proved Mr. Black to be a most enterprising farmer not only making a success of whatever he attempted in farming but he also undertook a great deal of public work. May I list a few of his undertakings:

In 1908 he was made Justice of the Peace

In 1911 he bought Red House Farm

In 1916 he bought Hardings Farm, Norton, near Red House.

In 1915-1918 he was elected a member of the East Suffolk Food Production Committee being Chairman in Charge of organising the usage of imported tractors and farm machinery during the war.

In 1919, together with Sam Sherwood, John Keeble and C C Smith they formed the East Suffolk Branch of the National Farmers' Union.

He was Chairman from 27th February of that year until 1934 and was County delegate to London for fifteen years.

In 1924 he became a member of the Elmswell Bacon Factory, Chairman from 1926 to 1934.

In 1934, he was appointed General Manager of the Pig Marketing Board for two years then Chairman of the Elmswell Bacon Factory to 1945.

From 1939 to 1945 he served on the Agricultural District
Committee.

In 1958 he was awarded the OBE for services to agriculture.

I have been told that on a small table in Mr. Black's
sitting room at Red House Farm there lay three well
thumbed books, namely the Holy Bible, a Dictionary and a
copy of Burns' Poems all of which I am sure contributed to
his success. Many agreed that he was a shrewd business man
with the dry sense of humour which is associated with
Scotland. I remember a prize-giving day at the Chadacre
Agricultural Institute near Bury St. Edmunds when, after the
speeches and the presentation of prizes by the late Lady
Iveagh and after tea a small group gathered to chat outside
the Institute. The group included the Principal Mr. Seward
and Mr. Black who had met on various occasions. "I don't
know", said Mr. Black, "that this college training is all that
necessary for Agriculture, I never went to no college and I
don't think I have done so badly." At which Mr. Seward
retorted, "Yes, we know, Mr. Black, the great successes you
have achieved in agriculture but I just cannot imagine what
you would have been had you had a college training." We
all laughed heartily, including Mr. Black.

It is not generally known that Mr. Black some years after
arriving at Red House Farm started a Stud of Hackney
Horses, breeding and showing them at local shows. I would
not be surprised if he brought the idea from Scotland as
there were some excellent Studs there at that time. Two of
the noted breeders were Major Miller of Balmano Castle,
Perth, and J Ernest Kerr, of Harveston Castle, Dollar. At
the Royal Highland and other leading shows the perfectly
driven hackney was a delight to watch and always one of the
greatest attractions. One of the finest specimens was
Knight Commander owned by Major Miller and I understand
that this horse was eventually sold to Holland for a very
good price. I have a friend in Fife who gets a great deal of
pleasure from breaking and selling hackneys. As in the case
of the draught-horse, mechanisation has taken over, still
there are people about who love to drive a hackney or a
pair. I am afraid David Black's hackneys fell on evil times.

During the First World War thousands of horses were used and the authorities came along and took four of his best, no wonder he decided to terminate that enterprise.

One scarcely ever sees a Suffolk Punch at work but at our local horse shows as many as fifty appear; when they all get together in the Grand Ring for the parade they are a splendid spectacle, all being chestnut in colour; we have many keen breeders. David Black's only son Tom and his three grandsons carry on the high standard of farming he set and the area they farm has now increased to over 1,700 acres. The three grandsons are all married, their families include eleven boys so the name Black is likely to continue in Bacton for many years. David Black died on 22nd February 1960, aged eighty five.

JOHN COWANS OF LAYER BRETON HALL, COLCHESTER

John was born in 1859, a few miles north of the Scottish border, the third of ten sons, eight of whom lived to exceed the age of eighty years. As a young man he spent most of his life with the Robinson family in North Northumberland where he got a good education in the management of cattle and sheep. He married in 1893 and took over the tenancy of Park Head Farm which was on the Trevelyan's Netherwitton Estate near Rothbury. Towards the end of the century part of the farm was taken to make a small reservoir thus upsetting the balance of the farm; this, coupled with medical advice that his wife would benefit from a milder climate influenced his decision to move south. So by train everything was transported to Corringham, near Tilbury on Major Whitmore's (Orsett Hall) Estate. John brought down many Scotch Blackfaced lambs to fatten on the marshland and their small joints found favour with the London butchers. All was going well when the sheep suddenly became ill and he was losing between ten and twenty a week. A carcass was taken to the London Veterinary College and the trouble diagnosed was a worm that could not then be treated. The College Principal came down to Corringham Hall and advised that he vacate the farm as soon as possible. Fortunately Mr. Cowans had the farm on a yearly tenancy and the advice was promptly taken. I have no doubt our able scientists have since discovered a remedy for this pest.

In 1910 he moved to Butley Abbey Farm near Woodbridge which in those days was about 3,000 acres comprising arable light land and heath together with the Orford (Kings) marshes. 1912-13 saw negotiations between Lord Rendlesham and the War Office whereby the Orford Marshes were compulsorily purchased to make the Orford Ness Airfield. Once again they upset the balance of the farm, so in September 1916 John left Butley Abbey and purchased Moat Hall, Layham near Hadleigh where he remained until the Autumn of 1925. I am privileged to have a catalogue of the Butley Abbey Farm agricultural sale of livestock etc; held on 21st September 1916 conducted by that witty auctioneer, Alfred Preston. The sale included thirty-six horses, four of which were hackneys. John loved a fast hackney which he drove regularly to and from Ipswich market. The sale of Butley Abbey also included eighty-five cattle, forty of them young milch cows besides 650 Suffolk sheep, ewes and lambs. There was also a large number of carriages, implements and the usual farm effects. The sale was held in the middle of the First World War and prices were good, it being a time when people depended on the British farmer for much of their food.

Wetheringsett Manor (about twelve miles north of Ipswich on the main Norwich road) was purchased by John in the Autumn of 1925, and after three months he received a very good offer for the property, this he accepted and on moving out in the spring of 1926, decided to retire from active farming and he moved to Church Farm, Snape. He very quickly became bored with retirement and looked around at various farms, ultimately purchasing Layer Breton Hall, Birch near Colchester. This was a farm of some 470 acres which had been farmed by Haslers, Dunmow Corn and Seed Merchants and was mostly tillage. They had greatly improved the land and on putting it down to grass it made excellent pasture for John's favoured 'dog and stick' farming. He was farming Layer Breton Hall when I was introduced to him at Bury Market by the late Arthur Forbes. He at once invited Mr. Forbes and me to visit him at his home, a date was arranged and we duly appeared. I shall never forget the welcome his wife and he gave us and the interest of that afternoon.

Farming was his life and he took a great pride in his farm, buildings were maintained in good repair, barns thatched and tarred. At Layer Breton Hall the road ran through the centre of the farm and every year the hedges were hand clipped the whole length of the farm on both sides of the road. Arthur Forbes and I admired his thriving cattle and sheep which were grazing lovely pastures of grasses and clovers. "Now," said John, "I have something special to show you." So we walked down to the entrance to his drive, there we saw a huge iron gate hung on a smart wooden post which appeared much too slender to support the gate for long. Arthur at once said, "How long do you think this post is going to take the strain?" "Ah! just look at this," said John, at the far bottom corner of the gate he had fixed a tiny wheel with a slight groove in the concrete of the road in which it ran. Consequently I would say it was taking more than half the weight of the gate. We three stood and viewed this cute invention. I can see John now, a man of fine stature though getting old, he threw back his shoulders and said with glee, "What do you think of that, friend Forbes?" Arthur who was never short of ideas himself, agreed it was good. This invention, and another of an up-to-date method of dipping sheep he had devised with oak fencing and concrete obviously gave him enormous pride. When his wife one day found the old shepherd creosoting the woodwork forming the pens, she commented it was a lot of money to spend on something that was of limited use. He replied, "One should live as if one is going to die tomorrow and farm as if one is going to live forever."

In 1937 the farm was compulsorily purchased by the South Essex Water Company to join part of the Abberton Reservoir required for the expansion of the Thameside development for Dagenham. Once again, with the centre of the farm taken, he was left with the higher ground on each side but he decided to continue as tenant.

I have mentioned that John was fond of a fast trotting hackney. When he farmed at Butley Abbey he had three neighbours who also farmed in that wide area between the rivers Alde and Deben, rivals who drove smart ponies and traps to market. Each one reckoned he had the best pony so there was friendly rivalry between them. One Tuesday as they were all about to leave Ipswich, John invited them to come to his house for tea before going home, "And the first to get to my place has the best pony." It was a distance of fifteen miles. Off they set more or less together, John keeping slightly in front and as he got near home, being out of sight of the others, he came to a partly secluded lane which ran from the main road down to his farm. Unnoticed he drove down this lane shortening the journey by three quarters of a mile. When the others arrived John had already unyoked and unharnessed his pony besides giving it water and food. "Now you know who has the best pony!" he teasingly called out. They were very doubtful how John could have managed the journey in such short time; after much leg pulling he eventually disclosed the secret.

In 1940 at the age of eighty-one the wartime restrictions were such that he was persuaded to call it a day. He moved to a cottage on an old friend's farm at Grafham near Huntingdon. Here he died on 30th November 1941 at the age of eighty-two. A man of character and charm! When he and his fellow countryman, Benjamin Black, who farmed at Rookery Farm, Ashfield, Bury St. Edmunds met in the market I found them most interesting to listen to.

ARCHIBALD LACY SCOTT OF BURY ST. EDMUNDS

I am very happy to write about Archibald Lacy Scott, the well known Bury St. Edmunds Auctioneer, who was a good friend to me, and who was especially encouraging and helpful when I wanted to farm in Suffolk.

Known as Archi to his family, close friends and associates, a Suffolk man born and bred. He was born on 15th September 1872, eldest son of Henry Lacy Scott and Emma. His father Henry was Mayor of Bury St. Edmunds for two years (1889 to 1891) and very enthusiastic about his Local Authority work.

Archi started his education at a small private school in Bury St. Edmunds and eventually obtained a Scholarship to King Edward VI's Grammar School in Bury St. Edmunds where his father and two brothers and at least three

Archibald Lacy Scott

subsequent brothers-in-law were educated also. On leaving school, Archi wished to become a solicitor and sat and passed the preliminary examination of the Law Society.

His father, however, was very anxious for him to join the firm (now Lacy Scott and Sons), and persuaded his son to abandon his aspiration for the law and join him in the firm of Auctioneers, Surveyors and Estate Agents which in fact Archi did. The firm had been founded by Henry Lacy Scott in July 1869 and there was little doubt that he wanted his son to carry on and it is highly likely that he needed that assistance.

Archi succumbed to the pressure, abandoned the law, and joined his father in about 1890 and during that decade passed his professional examinations of the then Surveyors' Institution, now the Royal Institution of Chartered Surveyors.

On joining the office, he found that owing to his father's great attachment to his public duties, no letter was allowed to be opened until Henry had completed his public activities, which meant 'after tea'. Archi did not care for this type of administration and dealt with the post on his arrival at the office, probably about 8.30 a.m. There was some altercation between father and son, the latter finally making his point and winning the battle. Incidentally on an occasion when the Lord Mayor of London invited every Mayor and Mayoress of the country to a function at the Mansion House, Henry was recorded in the reports as being "The Youngest Mayor of the Oldest Borough".

Archi soon began to increase the activities of the firm and with his leanings towards the Law, became one of the earlier authorities on Agricultural Law of that time, as it affected both Landlord and Tenant. At the same time he began to increase the firm's activities in the livestock market.

In 1903 Archi, who for some nine years previously lived in his bachelor's house adjoining the Abbots Bridge in Bury St. Edmunds, married Helen Norton of Hill House, Rickinghall. Helen was the daughter of the late Mr. Charles Thomas Norton and of Mrs. Louise Norton of Hill House, and had met her future husband through her eldest brother, a contemporary and friend of Archi's at the Grammar School.

She was one of a family of eleven and it is believed that occasionally they ran their own mixed hockey team. Archi and Helen hired Bridge House, Long Melford as a temporary house, but in fact remained there for twenty years, eventually moving permanently to Bury St. Edmunds in 1923.

Under Archi's ability, his father having died at the age of fifty-six in 1904, the firm had progressed and expanded. He became Managing Agent of the Belchamp Hall Estate in 1913, an Estate still managed by his son John. He also acquired on behalf of Sir John Aird, whose firm was responsible for the building of the first Aswam Dam, the Brandon Park Estate, which he managed until its realisation when Sir John moved to London.

During the First World War, Archi became a Captain in the Voluntary Training Corps. (V.T.C.) commanding the Long Melford and District section.

Although Archi disliked Local Authority work, he accepted, soon after settling in Long Melford, the Chairmanship of the Parish Council. He said later in life that he resigned after one year on account of the upsets he had in locating the four gas street lamps allotted to the parish through which the main Bury St. Edmunds to Sudbury Road covers some four miles or so. He said he made more enemies in that one year than during the rest of his life although there was no street lamp allocated near his own residence. He became also President of the Long Melford Football Club (known in those days as The Little Village) which, during his Presidency, won the Senior Suffolk Cup (prior to the establishment of Professional Clubs) on two occasions.

Turning to Archi's professional life, he served for twelve years on the Council of the Royal Institution of Chartered Surveyors. He also served on the Council of the Central Association of Agricultural Valuers and was elected President of this Society for 1943/44. He occupied the Presidential Chair of both the Suffolk and the Cambridge and Isle of Ely Valuers Associations. During the Second World War he was nominated by the Ministry of Agriculture and Food to the Pool Committee and was responsible for the payment to producers of livestock for all animals purchased by the Government in the County of Suffolk, for meat for distribution under the National Rationing Scheme.

He had four children, two daughters and two sons, both of the sons entered the business of Lacy Scott and Sons with their father's younger brother, Reginald, who had joined the firm in the early 1900s. Both of Archi's sons have followed in his footsteps, each having served on the General Council or Regional Council of the Royal Institution whilst the younger has passed through the Presidential Chair of the Central Association of Agricultural Valuers. They have both been elected Presidents of the Valuers Association on which their father had held a similar position. His elder son succeeded him on the Pool Committee and subsequently on the cessation of the rationing of food, served on the Livestock Auctioneers Markets Committee for England and Wales being Chairman for a number of years. Archi was an experienced Aricultural Arbitrator, and again both his sons have followed him in a similar capacity.

It was his ability as an Auctioneer and Valuer of live and dead farming stock on which Archi and I had many discussions in his private room after market on a Wednesday. One day I was approached by a farmer friend who had three farms some distance apart. He said as he was getting old he would like to know the value of his livestock and implements on the farms. He suggested Archi Lacy Scott as valuer but as many of his cattle and sheep had been bred near or north of the Border, he thought I would be an asset in helping him in fixing their value. Archi was very pleased that I should assist him in the valuation on the three farms. It took us two days to complete the job. There was a large dairy herd and many store cattle of various ages and many hundreds of sheep besides lots of implements. We each had our separate note book and while we discussed the merits of each bunch of cattle and sheep together, we stepped apart and noted our individual ideas of the value of each lot. On an odd occasion there was a pound or two between us but on more than one lot our values tallied. On reading the long list of values, the old gentleman was very pleased, though he had one complaint. We had under-estimated the value of a bunch of some twelve Cumberland-bred short-horn eighteen-month old steers he had bought recently by £2 each. These were very nice cattle, perhaps we were a little wrong, but there was the possiblity that he paid a wee bit too much for the sake of being the owner of a good animal as has sometimes happened to me. However, this made little difference to his total assets. On the way home, I was gratified when Archi said to me "You've missed your vocation, George." May I mention that Archi's elder son, Henry, and I were close friends from the time he entered the firm of Lacy Scott and Sons. A young man full of energy and drive; it was due to his ability that this firm has the biggest store sheep and lamb sales in East Anglia.

Archi died on 25th November 1953, aged eighty-one.

One of Lacy Scott and Sons' Store
Sheep and Lamb sales

CHAPTER VIII

HALL FARM, STANTON, BURY ST EDMUNDS

The methods of finding a living by livestock farming in East Anglia, especially cattle and sheep, I found differed considerably from what I had been accustomed to in Scotland, and the same could be said of arable farming.

When my brother and I arrived in the autumn of 1925 on a yearly tenancy to a heavy land farm of 218 acres in West Suffolk, half being grass, the other half arable, we decided to graze the grassland with a dairy herd of thirty milk cows plus 150 Cheviot ewes which we brought from Scotland. We also brought six Clydesdale horses and implements to farm the arable side. Tractors were just starting to appear on the larger farms; milking machines too were just coming on the market and we purchased a two-unit plant two years later.

As there had been no sheep on this farm since "no-one knew when," our Cheviots thrived and produced a nice crop of lambs in the spring. The cows, too, were a success in spite of the fact that part of their winter diet the first year was barley straw made more appetising by sprinkling diluted treacle over it in the mangers.

It was the arable side of the farm that gave us the bigger worries. Our Suffolk horsemen did not cog in well with our Scottish Clydesdales as they tried to grade the horses down to a lower gear than they had been accustomed to. This the horses resented so co-operation was not of the highest standard.

That autumn, owing to rain, we had difficulty with the drilling of our winter wheat and beans; when there were a few dry days the heavy land was slow in drying out. We had agreed the tenancy of the farm in the previous June when there had been a nice spell of dry weather. Every field had looked shipshape to the naked eye but the fact was, as we eventually realised, we had hired a badly drained farm. As we had been accustomed to sloping land in Scotland, perhaps we were ignorant of the value and necessity of good tile drains on this heavy land. This was very disappointing to my wife, my brother and myself as we were settling in nicely to our new environment and making many friends. We had agreed a fair rent but why should we have to pipe-drain most of the owner's property to get the necessary results? So my brother and I decided to give a year's notice to quit the farm. The owner, who had farmed this land before we arrived, knew perfectly well the condition of the farm but made no offer to assist us to put the matter right. Perhaps it was our fault in failing to take the advice expressed by our National Poet to a young friend:

> "Conceal yourself as weel's ye can
> Frae critical dissection,
> But keek thro' ev'ry other man
> Wi' sharpened sly inspection."

So we tendered our notice to quit the farm at the end of the second year, my wife and I going to a bigger light land farm in Norfolk taking the sheep with us and leaving my brother with the cows to complete the tenancy before joining up with us in Norfolk.

Before I cease to comment on this heavy land farm may I mention some of the conditions of entry at that time. Nearly all land was farmed on the four-course shift as there were no weed-killing sprays or insecticides in those days. To help keep farms reasonably clean about one quarter of the arable acreage each year was made a long fallow. This entailed three times ploughing during the spring and summer and twice cultivating. Should one happen to be an outgoing tenant one had to give the dates each operation was completed. The tenant could make no claim against the landlord for his overgrown hedges and full ditches while the landlord could claim against the tenant on vacating the farm.

On entry to the farm the tenant was responsible for the threshing of the owner's crop, getting the straw in payment. He was also responsible for the delivery of the grain up to a distance of ten miles. A tenant-farmer taking over from the landlord would have been well advised to have an official record of the condition of the farm at entry.

The fattening of cattle in yards seemed to be much more laborious than that practised in Scotland. Owing to the warm climate and the low rainfall in East Anglia the growing of swedes and turnips was not satisfactory; mangolds, however, make a good root crop. Before mechanical cleaners came on the market these had to be cleaned by hand before being ground up then added to a big heap of damped chaff on the barn floor together with a balanced ration of ground barley and beans. Then the resulting mixture was turned over three times before being fed to the cattle in the mangers. The growing of mangolds has long been stopped and silage has taken over with a balanced concentrate fed separately in the mangers.

The feeding facilities too have greatly improved. In my early days in East Anglia there was only one gate into many of the cattle yards; the yardman had to struggle with his bushel of feed through the width of the yards to reach the mangers. Now cattle are fed from the outer wall of the yard by a side-delivery feed box drawn and driven by a tractor.

Sheep were kept on many farms when I arrived in the area in 1925. The system adopted also entailed much labour, close-folding being the method, with enough feed for the flock for one day. This was a good method of manuring the land regularly. However, labour and equipment eventually became too expensive and one seldom sees a folded flock today; in fact sheep have decreased considerably throughout East Anglia. Only a few of the natives have adopted the ley farming system which I am sure is still profitable. I kept sheep for many years by this method.

CHAPTER IX

WATER END FARM, STANFORD, NORFOLK

Throughout the twelve years we farmed in Norfolk, 1926-1938, dairying and sheep were our principal sources of income. Prices of all classes of grain were so low that wholly arable farming was unprofitable and even ruinous. We only ploughed an acreage necessary for straw and roots for winter feed and litter for our milking herd, besides an acreage of mangolds for the ewes before and after lambing.

The grassy pastures which nearly encircled the thirty acre lake provided enough feed in spite of there being three very hot summers. With the use of a two-unit milking machine we found we could milk twenty cows an hour; by hand one had to be good to keep up an average of eight per hour, so this proved a valuable investment.

The most important event of these twelve years was the arrival of our son Alastair.

Our flock of 300 Border Cheviots throve on this very light land farm where sheep had not been kept for many years previously. As these sheep roamed over an area of some 250 acres, to shepherd them a well trained Border Collie was necessary. Using Suffolk Rams we arranged the lambing to start about 20th March. By the first week in July the first lot was ready for the fat market at Bury St. Edmunds, following on with twenty or so each week. These quality lightweight lambs found favour with the local butchers so they sold readily.

After about five years in partnership with my brother he left to farm on his own, a grass farm in Essex which he grazed with sheep and suckler cows. From then on I had to employ a cowman. Arthur Walker was an excellent chap for using the milking machines and rearing calves.

My landlord, Lord Walsingham, owned a large area of land. Some fifty per cent of it was light land, not productive enough as a purely arable proposition; such was the farm I had. The previous tenant who farmed it on the four-course shift had given up. His Lordship, who was highly respected by his tenantry, fully realised the difficulties of farming this class of land when prices of grain were low as they were throughout the 1930s. No doubt he noticed I kept a fair number of cattle and sheep and when he told me, "Just farm the farm as you wish," this suited me. I had been taught to work by a father who lived in Victorian times, in a decent, good and friendly society, long before strikes were thought about. Strikes, I consider, only benefit a few after upsetting a great many.

During the years ahead there was considerable unrest in Europe. Germany under Hitler was causing so much trouble that one day war would be inevitable. As I had farming experience throughout the First World War when people had to depend on home agriculture for much of their living I felt I ought to move to a more productive farm. I had threatened to leave on a previous occasion but through the persuasive ability of Lord Walsingham I had been induced to stay. However, I was now determined to terminate my lease in the Autumn of 1938.

As I have mentioned, while times were difficult throughout these twelve years, no-one having much money to spare, the social life of the parish was not neglected. The village people were friendly and co-operative and we joined in various activities. The children, too, were not forgotten.

Our farm was situated between the village and the lake so we were never short of wildlife around us. Rabbits were numerous on the heathland adjoining the farm which was encircled by rabbit netting. I kept a rabbit catcher busy for ten months of the year so rabbits did not become too numerous and they invariably paid the rent of the farm. This was, of course, long before myxomatosis took control.

On the lake, which was known as Stanford Watering, many specimens of wild birds assembled throughout the year. There were swans, at least one pair came to nest each year and rear their young. There was a variety of duck, chiefly mallard; a number of coot stayed the winter. Herons, too, often paid a visit as there were many fish in the lake, tench, roach, pike and many other coarse fish. I have been told that a pike weighing 22 lbs has been caught from this Watering.

A small boat was kept in the boathouse by the lake and it was lent to anyone asking permission to fish. However, I once saw it used for a very different purpose. One autumn there was a meet of the Norfolk Staghounds. A number of deer I understand were kept in a park in the vicinity of Norwich. For the sport one strong stag was selected, taken in a motor van well into the country and then released. After it had a good start the hounds were let loose from a larger van in which they had travelled to the meet. By mid-afternoon that day the stag arrived at Stanford Watering and went right in until it reached about the middle of the thirty acre lake and there it stood. The water being shallow, its head, neck and the ridge of its back could be seen. The hounds eventually arrived but did not fancy entering the water; no doubt the scent was cut off. I do not remember anyone arriving on horseback but the two vans eventually appeared. Two men with a rope rowed out in the boat, lassoed the deer, brought it back to the edge of the lake, put it in the van and took it back to join its mates in the park near Norwich. One cannot be sure how far that deer had run but I would say quite thirty miles.

Another event occurred at the Watering the following summer. A Norfolk Wildlife Club, some twelve persons, arrived to get to the lake. From the road they had to walk over one of my grassy pastures and, as they approached the edge, up flew an osprey which circled over their heads. This certainly had 'made their day' as was mentioned in the local newspaper two days later.

As in many other dairy farming families it became no hardship, nor even a desperate effort, to wake up at 4.30 each morning, dress and rush down to make a cup of tea and be in the cowshed by 5.0 a.m. The milk had to be transported to Thetford Station, a distance of seven miles in our Ford T Model truck to catch the 8.0 a.m. train for London; one must never be late.

In the summer months my Border Collie, Scot was very handy for rounding up the cows so that we got them quickly though quietly into the cowshed. One clear Sunday morning the cows were grazing the pasture on the far side of the lake which extended close up to the village; a road ran along the end of the lake with a gate at the further end. When I got to the gate I sent Scot off to round up the cows. Somehow he missed two which had been lying against the hedge near the village. When I saw this I shouted "Scot man ye're daft," as I gave him his "go back" whistle. During the week I happened to meet Dick Goss who said, "I am sorry to hear, Mr. Anderson, that your dog Scot has gone daft. Last Sunday morning I was awake with my window open and I heard you plainly say "Scot man ye're daft." I got that one back from several of the village folks during the week.

CHAPTER X

BOULGE HALL FARM, WOODBRIDGE

The year 1937 had gone and I had already tendered my notice to quit Water End Farm in the autumn of 1938. My wife and I and son Alastair, who was then seven years old, were in search of a new home. As prices of grain were still low it was a farm of a reasonable amount of pasture land with a cowshed that would suit me best and with a few acres to spare for sheep.

Mr. Forbes and his son Duncan, farming near me in Norfolk, had often talked of East Suffolk where they had farmed for a number of years long before I arrived and had made many friends. To farm in that part of Suffolk I felt would suit my wife and me, so I kept my ear "close to the ground" for any information of likely farms to let in that area. Eventually a number came to my notice. I viewed four; of these Boulge Hall Farm was most likely to suit me, there being 200 acres of pasture and a cowshed to tie up twenty cows. It belonged to Sir Robert White of Boulge Hall and had been his Home Farm for many years, supplying the Hall with dairy produce and eggs. His farm manager who lived in the farmhouse decided to retire and as Sir Robert himself was not a young man, he decided to let the farm. I made application to become tenant of the farm and was eventually accepted.

Living thirty miles away in Norfolk many people wondered how I came to be chosen. Sir Robert was not interested in my scholastic attainments or in my social position but it was my experience as a farmer that satisfied him. Since I left the Borders it has been brought home to me over these many years, during which I have been in contact with people of much higher education and position, that Scotland's National Poet aptly summed up the situation when he wrote "A man's a man for a' that."

Boulge Hall Suffolk, demolished 1956

On 11th October 1938 we moved 'lock, stock and barrel' to our new home in the parish of Boulge. It is a small parish with no shop, no pub but a very nice wee Church. Sir Robert's agent, Mr. Arnold Forster, realised that improvements were needed to the farmhouse and that I required an extension to the cowshed as our herd had now increased to forty cows, so builders were in and around the house until Christmas of that year.

The majority of the arable land of the farm is of a heavy loam over a chalky-clay sub-soil, known in those days as a "Wheat and Bean" farm, so our first job was to get these planted. At intervals during the winter months we threshed Sir Robert's crop which conisted of thirteen large oblong stacks, beautifully thatched in the East Anglian method. Wheat straw was pulled from a well-wetted heap and put between a "V" shaped branch so that it could be carried up the ladder and placed in layers called yellums on the roof of the stack, wooden broaches and binder-string being used to keep the thatch secure. The wooden broaches were cut from hazel, pointed at one end and notched a few inches from the other. These eighteen inch broaches were driven horizontally into the stack and the binder-twine was firmly secured to the notched end and passed over the yellums to keep the thatch in place. This method certainly kept the stacks dry. These stacks of wheat, barley and beans were built large enough for a full day's threshing in the winter months requiring ten men.

Less than a year after our arrival at Boulge we were at war with Germany. Being situated a few miles from the east coast, the blackout was very important as we were soon to get many German planes over during the hours of darkness. I was appointed Air-raid Warden for the parish; my principal job was to see that the regulations were adhered to.

On the farm we were producing as much food as possible; some of the pasture land was ploughed. Our chief crops were wheat, barley, sugar beet, with kale, hay and eventually silage for the production of winter milk. My Kerryhill ewes did well, their fat lambs by a Suffolk ram were in demand by the local butchers.

When hostilities were over I stuck to the same method of

farming. I had not forgotten the disastrous drop in farm prices in 1921 shortly after the First World War and the near hopeless survival of arable farming throughout the awful 1930s.

It was by sheep and cows that we survived, so I carried on milking a herd of Friesians by purchasing well-bred bulls, paying attention to conformation of the animals as well as quantity of milk and high butterfat. I eventually bred a very useful herd. This was borne out by the good prices I got for surplus heifers in Ipswich Market, helped by the way they were shown by my cowman George Hunt. George would stand by them at the market until they were sold; he was always on the spot to give particulars to prospective buyers. Having sold them well, he thoroughly enjoyed his pint afterwards in the inn nearby.

We reared all the calves, selling the fat steers as barley-beef around fourteen months, on two occasions winning the Cup for the Best Butchers Bullock at the Wickham Market Christmas Fatstock Show and Sale. It is several years since a Friesian gained that honour, the exotic breeds now taking over.

When our son Alastair joined me as a partner we increased the milking herd to one hundred after building a parlour with a five-a-side milking unit which one man could manage. We made grass and maize silage for the winter feed.

From 1956 we started to grow crops for the deep-freeze trade, peas, dwarf beans and brussel sprouts. This meant the ploughing up of pasture land and the squeezing out of my beloved sheep. However, I had the grazing of the Suffolk Show ground just eight miles away for fourteen years. Each year I bought cross-bred ewe lambs and sold them as shearlings the following August. As I grew older I felt my shepherding days were over, so I finally gave up the show-ground grazing.

We carried on the method of farming I have mentioned for several years, in fact up to 1980. By that time milk had become over-produced and as feeding stuffs had become more expensive owing to increased prices of grain, we decided to sell our dairy herd and change our system of farming. Now, apart from one pasture field for my grand-daughter's horses, the whole of the farm is geared to arable farming.

As I have mentioned, Boulge, the parish in which we live, is small, situated ten miles from Ipswich where there was an excellent livestock market, and four miles from Wickham Market where there is a similar weekly market, together with an auction sale of vegetables, eggs and all classes of furniture. Woodbridge is three miles away, situated on the River Deben some ten miles from the sea; the town is built on sloping ground to the east and makes a beautiful picture in summertime, as one approaches it by boat up the tidal Deben river. Woodbridge also has a famous Yacht Club. There is no major industry in the town which is a pleasant one for shopping.

An interesting feature of Woodbridge is the Tide Mill. It is almost two hundred years old and if you had been an inhabitant of Woodbridge in the eighteenth century you would have been familiar with a mill on that very spot. The present structure was the first of its kind to be built in England, in 1793.

The Mill Pond has been restored and once more the tide fills it twice in twenty-four hours. In the past the head of water in the pond was responsible for driving the great wooden wheel. Two hours before low tide the water thundered out at about the middle of the wheel but as the level of the pond dropped the sluice-gates were opened and the water was released much lower down on the wheel; to the miller this was forecast 'shot' and 'undershot'. In turn it rotated the massive grinding stones. The miller and his family must have had to suffer a great deal of noise and his working hours were governed by the tides.

The Mill's great voice was silenced in 1957 when the 22-inch square beam of oak, which was the shaft, cracked. From 1957 to 1968 it remained derelict but then the mill was rescued by a generous benefactor who gave it to the town. Subsequently a Trust was set up and now, although its working life is ended, visitors can see the Tide Mill as it was in the eighteenth century.

It was directly opposite Woodbridge, on rising ground on the left bank of the River Deben known as Sutton Hoo, that excavations were made in 1939 which led to the discovery of

Woodbridge Tide Mill from across the Harbour

the royal Ship, the remains of a long clinker-built boat. In this ship were placed all the necessities the Anglians believed their king would require in the next world. This was an indication of the pagan element which existed in East Anglia at that time, thought to be around 700 AD. The huge excavations of very sandy soil are not seen from the town, owing to a nineteenth century plantation. The 'Sutton Hoo Ship' as it is known, is said to be the archaeological find of the century.

Throughout Britain the Spring of 1983 was one of the coldest and wettest in living memory. Arable farm work in the South, especially on heavy land was completely bogged down and these conditions existed for at least seven weeks, consequently spring work such as the planting of potatoes, sugar beet and drilling of peas for the deep freeze trade were so late that an average crop seemed extremely unlikely. My thoughts went back to the lambing season on the hills in Scotland. I fully appreciated the trying times the shepherds would have, a cold time at lambing is bad but when it is accompanied by driving rain nothing can be more trying to the survival of new born lambs.

I value the correspondence I have received from time to time from relatives of some of the Scottish shepherds I knew so well. I am pleased to show this photograph of Mitt Little, 'Roughlee', Bonchester Bridge, Roxburghshire standing by a dry stone wall by the sheep pens and wearing the familiar shepherd's wide brimmed tweed hat, admiring a pen of his beloved Cheviots. His Border Collie is in the background.

During that long cold wet time, I was sitting alone one night in front of my grate fire, eleven o'clock had struck, the rain kept battering on the windows and as I sat there watching the dying embers in the grate, I thought of the difficulties we were in on the farm. All classes of farm machinery were bogged down and the season for planting spring crops was becoming 'well spent'. We had rather a large acreage of peas and sugar beet besides a smaller acreage of spring barley to plant. As I sat gazing my thoughts sped back to my youth. A Border Hill farmer I knew who wrote weekly on Farming Topics to a famous Border Newspaper sometimes got inspiration from watching deein' embers when he was sitting up with a calvin' quey -

Group of Cheviot sheep shepherded by Mitt Little

(heifer). In my case it was starting to come true, I collected a writing pad, a pen and set off up to bed. After tucking myself in, sitting up I wrote these lines:-

I mind it weel in yester year
When I was young and blate, (1)
The first sheep that I had to shear,
I was in a trauchled (2) state

The Squire, he showed me how to start
And how to hold my ewe,
But not a word did he impart
On how to dicht (3) ma'broo.

Sweat, it trickled in ma' ee' (4)
Too weel, I couldna see,
Carefully I sheared that sheep
With that you will agree.

I clippit and I snippit
Producing' lots o' oo (5)
I felt I was getting mair (6)
Than the man wha clipped the Soo. (7)

(1) shy;　(2) worried;　(3) wipe brow;　(4) eye;　(5) wool;　(6) more;　(7) sow.

Boulge Church, dedicated to St. Michael and All Angels, stands in the fields. It is easily seen from the Bredfield to Debach road. To get to it one takes the concrete path on the left of the Bredfield to Debach road, eventually arriving at an avenue of beech trees which leads to the Church. The Churchyard contains the grave of Edward FitzGerald (1809-1883). This English poet was noted particularly for his translation of the Rubaiyat of Omar Khayyam written in 1859. Roses from Persia have been planted from time to time on his grave at Boulge, the last being sent by the Ambassador of Iran. June 14th 1983 being the centenary of his death, many people from various parts of the world found their way to visit his grave.

In the month of June the Churchyard resembles a

Interior of Boulge Church,
St. Michael and all Angels, Suffolk
Church Warden since 1940

meadow carpeted with flowering grasses, buttercups, ox-eye daisies, white and red clover and speedwell. These summer flowers replace in their season, snowdrops, daffodils, primroses, cowslips and bluebells. The Church is unique in its sylvan setting of dappled shade, surrounded by cornfields. It has an active life with worship every Sunday. At Christmas it is decked with holly and ivy; hundreds of twinkling candles fill the ancient Church with a warm golden light and the strains of age-old carols can be heard on the cold night air. Harvest also sees the Church full of people jostling for seats among the vegetables, dahlias and chrysanthemums. The produce is distributed while it is still fresh to local needy folks and the Almshouses in the nearby town of Ipswich.

CHAPTER XI

EPILOGUE

As I have now spent sixty years of my ninety in East Anglia, my dialect seems to have changed to English. However, when I chance to meet a complete stranger the conversation is generally of short duration before I am told, "You are Scottish," I find it is no use arguing, that I ain't!

In looking back on my long life I realise that most of the worthwhile things in it are connected with friendship. The greatest disappointment to my brother and me was having to leave our native Borderland to fulfil our ambition to become farmers. Having started over a hundred miles away in 1920, when prices seemed stable, then in 1921 to be badly let down by politicians in whom we had pinned our faith, we soon discovered the only way to combat the difficulties was hard work and rigid economy. Towards the end of our tenancy of Coulsknowe while circumstances had made these five years hard going, had it not been for the help and sympathy of farming friends we had made during that period, we could so easily have been down-and-out. I make no apology for quoting these lines from Shakespeare again, "There is a divinity that shapes our ends, rough-hew them how we will."

We never regretted the move to farm in East Anglia as most of the land can be adapted to alternative methods of farming.

On moving to East Anglia, Friesian Cattle became our chief interest and we were successful in breeding prize winning bulls and cows. Scotch Cheviot sheep we found did well and they were also suitable for the training of .my Border Collies though one of the best I bought untrained from J H Thorpe - a daughter of his 'Jess' which was International Champion in 1931. I ran 'Fly' in many of the East Anglian Sheep-Dog Society Trials and won a number of

As President of the Woodbridge Horse Show
presenting the cup for the Champion Mare in 1982

prizes. Suffolk horses, however, continue to give me the greatest livestock interest, even today, though they are not required for assisting in much farm work. It is gratifying to see so many East Anglian farmers with a real love for a Suffolk Punch, consequently one finds many farmers with one or two and there are still studs of ten to twenty horses throughout the area. There are classes at all our Agricultural Shows which create much interest.

The draught horse, behold him, how kind and domestic
To one who has ploughed many acres of yore,
The Suffolk Punch so strong and majestic,
The pride of the Show Ring and true to the core.

One of the best Suffolk Colt foals was born in February 1983, bred and exhibited by Michael Becher who farms near Framlingham. At all our leading Agricultural Shows, including the Royal, this foal has taken First Prize. Michael, whose prefix for the Suffolk animals he breeds is 'Cherrytrees', has complimented me by registering this foal in the Stud Book in my name viz. 'Cherrytrees George Murray'.

When we arrived in East Anglia in 1925 prices of all classes of grain were low and kept dropping, so we made livestock, dairying and breeding sheep our principal sources of income. Eventually after a number of years these became less economic, grain prices having improved. Apart from a small acreage our farmland is now arable and we find we are reaping the benefit of our previous livestock farming. We loved our cows and sheep, but one must get out of the rut, if the change is likely to be more beneficial. My active interest however, is now on the wane. "One cannot halt the march of time nor stay the passing years." The time has come when younger shoulders must take the strain and I am happy that my son Alastair and grandson, Robby, are coping with the up-to-date methods of farming.

Signing my first book at the Suffolk Show 1982

Writing my second book

Cutting my cake on 80th Birthday

Talking to the Piper on my 90th birthday

"Cherry Trees George Murray", with his mother, my grand-daughter, Judith and me.

"Cherry Trees George Murray" held by Alastair

THE JOY OF LIFE

As a wee bit tender laddie I toddled on the hills,
With my kindly father close at hand to guard me frae all
ills,
He gently found the hollow where the lark had laid her eggs,
While her silvery song cascaded doon from far aboon our
heads,
The plaintive call of whaup was first music tae my ear,
Those breezy golden far off days are full of memories dear.

As a happy Border Shepherd I worked from morn till eve,
Mother and brother shared the life I hoped I'd never leave,
I danced with young folks in the glens and praised our
Scottish Bard,
Our sheep and lambs throve well our hearts were glad, tho'
work was hard.
To talk and laugh with my good friends
I strode o'e brae and moor,
And I found my bonnie gifted bride in the hills of
Lammermuir.

Without his canine helpers no shepherd could survive,
Roy, Tim and Scot, Fly, Nell and Bess and many more
beside,
Tw'a Border Collies still I have, with my retirement shared,
No sheep or stock to work upon but still, like me, they're
spared,
With feline grace and crouching form, they gathered up the
sheep,
Which were gently guided o'er the braes or thro' the
gullies deep.

With whiskers stiff - wi' icicles and paws shod hard with
snow,
By blizzard wild, - both blinded, my dog and I would go,
To seek the missing sheep in snowdrifts deep and white,
The faithful clever dog would find them tho' hidden from my

sight,
I was but ten when first I worked a faithful loving friend,
And I'll maintain such friendships until the long roads end.

Far frae the Border noo I live in Suffolk's sunny clime,
The Friesian herd, the Suffolk Punch, and Suffolk sheep
were mine,
I loved them weel but they have gone, I've golden wheat
instead,
It's growin' fine, where on green grass contentedly they fed,
I've seen through many happy years the changes that life
sends,
And the greatest joy that I have now, is the love of all my
friends.

G.M.A.